Jim Arnosky

Rabbits & Raindrops

SCHOLASTIC INC.
New York Toronto London Auckland Sydney
Mexico City New Delhi Hong Kong

ISBN 0-439-06171-7

Copyright © 1997 by Jim Arnosky.
All rights reserved. Published by Scholastic Inc.,
555 Broadway, New York, NY 10012,
by arrangement with G.P. Putnam's Sons, a division of
The Putnam & Grosset Group. SCHOLASTIC and associated logos
are trademarks and/or registered trademarks of Scholastic Inc.

12 11 10   0 1 2 3 4/0

Printed in the U.S.A.   14

First Scholastic printing, April 1999

Book designed by Patrick Collins.

Text set in Horley Old Style

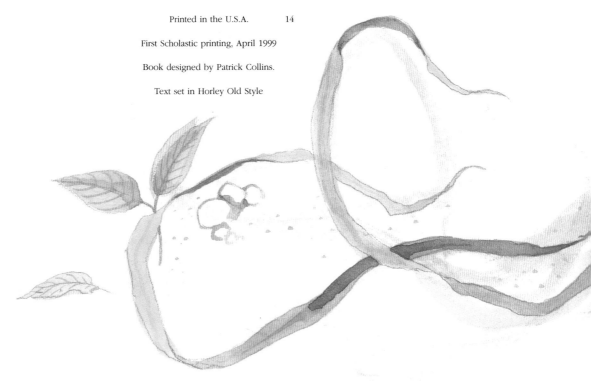

This book is dedicated to
Darren.

Mother rabbit sits
by her nest

under a hedge
at the edge
of green lawn.

Her five babies are ready
to climb out of the nest
for the first time.

Mother rabbit hops out
into the bright sunlight,

onto the green grass.

One after another,
the five baby rabbits
hop out onto the lawn.

They nibble clover
blossoms and leaves.

They meet grasshoppers,
spiders, and bees.

All of a sudden
the sky turns dark,
and big, heavy raindrops
begin to fall.

A rabbit's fur is not waterproof.
Baby rabbits can become
soaked, and catch cold.

So Mother rabbit hurries her babies back under the hedge.

From their dry shelter,
five baby rabbits
watch the rain pouring down.

A butterfly flutters in
under the hedge,
and rests on a dry leaf.